Now They All Have
Window Seats!

Now They All Have Window Seats!

A Reynolds Unwrapped Tribute to Fatherhood

Dan Reynolds

**Andrews McMeel
Publishing**

Kansas City

Now They All Have Window Seats!

04 05 06 07 08 WKT 10 9 8 7 6 5 4 3 2

ISBN: 0-7407-4200-0

Library of Congress Control Number: 2003113020

www.reynoldsunwrapped.com
e-mail: dreynol3@twcny.rr.com

Attention: Schools and Businesses

Andrews McMeel books are available at quantity discounts with bulk purchase for educational, business, or sales promotional use. For information, please write to: Special Sales Department, Andrews McMeel Publishing, 4520 Main Street, Kansas City, Missouri 64111.

I'd like to dedicate this book to all the fathers
who died both on September 11, 2001,
and during the war with Iraq.

PREFACE

I started cartooning almost immediately after my oldest son was born. I now have four sons and I've never stopped drawing. It has been very rewarding over the last thirteen years to see all of my children following my lead. All of them not just trying to be like Dad, but developing their own creative powers.

For many years, none of us understood each other's work. The kids and I would look at one another's finished works and say in unison, "What is it?" To my children, I wasn't a professional cartoonist with nationally selling books, greeting cards, and regular appearances in *Reader's Digest*—I was just "Daddy," a father who likes to draw neat pictures. They've learned about cartooning by example. I've learned about being a kid at heart from watching them.

When their formative years are all over, I hope my children have learned something else by example—how to be a dad who loves his kids.

"It's not easy raising kids today. You have to be both mother AND father to them."

"I don't like your altitude, mister. Go to your hangar. You're grounded."

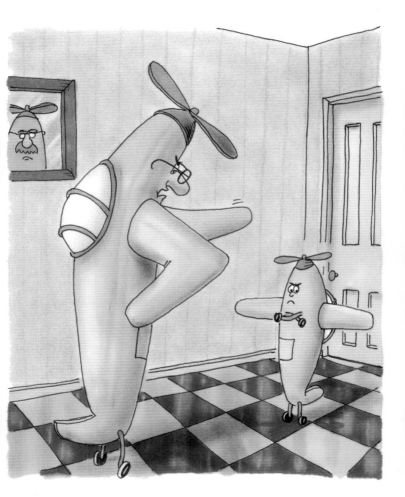

"Your father will be so surprised
I installed the new windows."

Joe's clothes dated him.

Extreme Comb-overs . . .

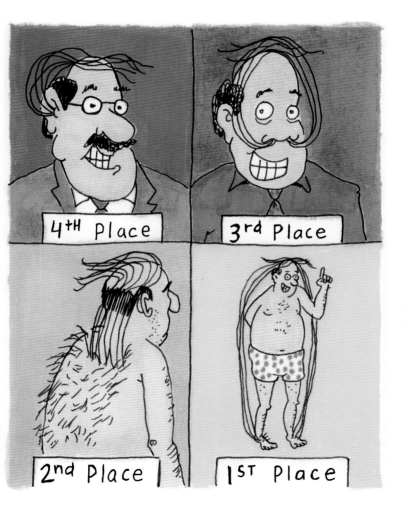

Ironically, at the same moment his wife goes into labor, Ronnie experiences his own contractions.

CAN'T...   WON'T...

MUSN'T...

SHOULDN'T...

"Let that be a lesson to you, son. . . . Crack kills."

"Hi, Daddy."

IN CASE OF
EMERGENCY
BREAK GLASS

The Dogfather

"It all began when I was just a kid."

Mozart as a child

New dad

"Don't worry. It's just a 'phrase' they're going through."

NO!
NO! NO!

"I think we need an image makeover."

Parrot families

"Waiter, we ordered our porridge hot, cold, and juuusst right. You brought us pease-porridge hot, pease-porridge cold, and pease-porridge in the pot, *NINE* days old."

"He gets that from YOUR
side of the family."

"What's the matter with you, son? You left the barn door closed again. Were you brought up in a house?"